Simply Science

READ ALOUD

Level 2 UNIT 6 Earth Science

Learning About Space

SRA

Columbus, OH

Cover Photo Credits: **(l)** © PhotoDisc/Getty Images, Inc.; **(c)** © Dennis di Cicco/CORBIS; **(r)** © NASA/Roger Ressmeyer/CORBIS.

SRAonline.com

Copyright © 2009 by SRA/McGraw-Hill.

All rights reserved. No part of this publication may be reproduced or distributed in any form or by any means, or stored in a database or retrieval system, without the prior written consent of The McGraw-Hill Companies, Inc., including, but not limited to, network storage or transmission, or broadcast for distance learning.

Printed in Mexico.

Send all inquiries to this address:
SRA/McGraw-Hill
4400 Easton Commons
Columbus, OH 43219

ISBN: 978-0-07-622465-4
MHID: 0-07-622465-1

1 2 3 4 5 6 7 8 9 RRM 15 14 13 12 11 10 09 08

The McGraw·Hill Companies

Contents

Earth Science — **Fiction**

Janie's Space Journey 4

Earth Science — **Nonfiction**

Earth in Space 14

Unit 6 • Vocabulary

axis line through the center of a spinning object

constellation star pattern that makes a picture

light kind of energy that lets us see

orbit to move around another object

planet object that travels around the sun

reflect to bounce light off an object

Earth Science Fiction

Janie's Space Journey

Janie stepped onto the launch pad with her parents. Janie and her parents were moving to the planet Nina on the other side of the galaxy! They would be gone for a whole year. Janie wondered how different Nina would be from Earth.

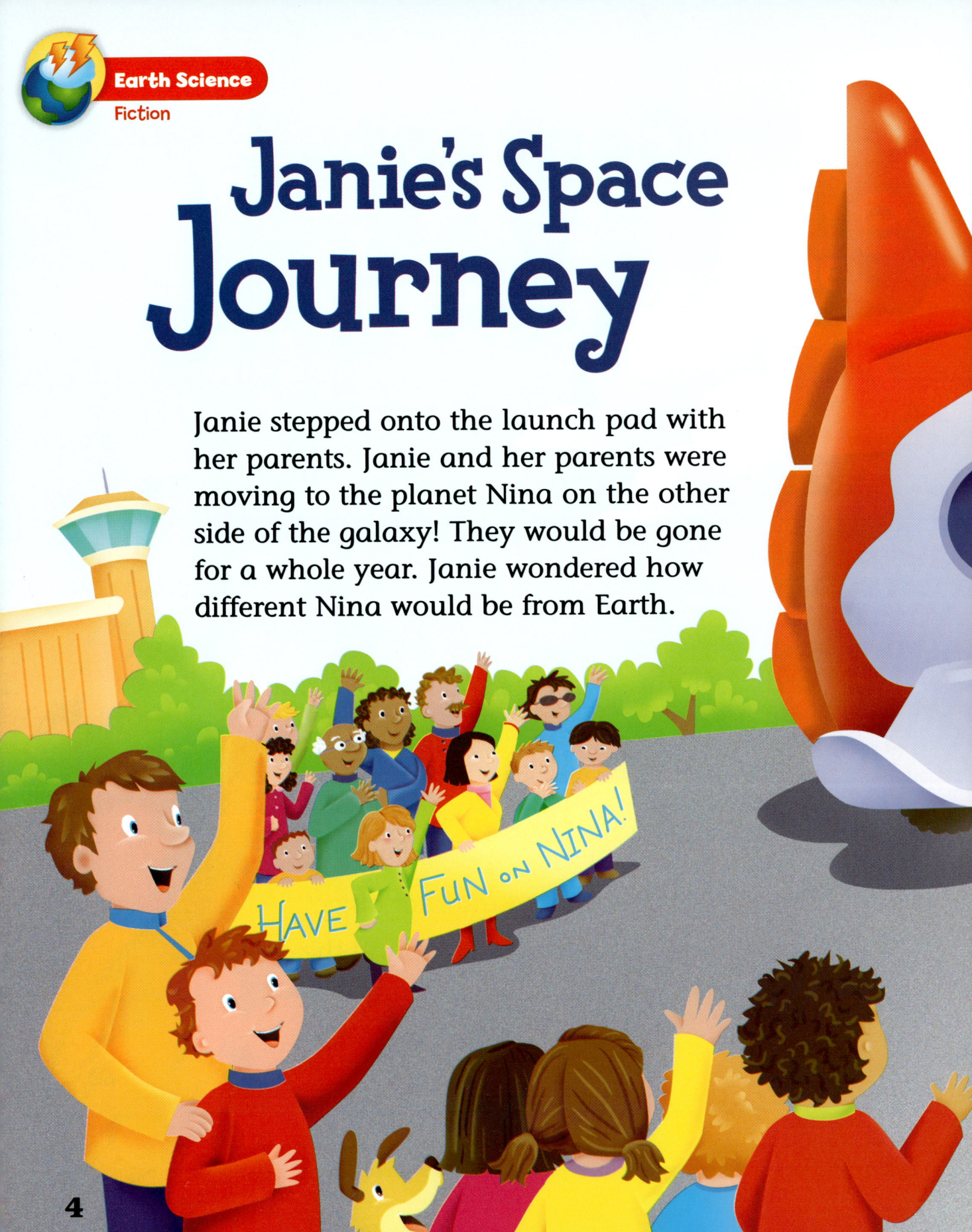

Janie's friend Joey and his father were there to say goodbye. "I'll see you soon!" Joey hollered.

Janie nodded and waved goodbye as she boarded the SPACER 3000.

Minutes later, the shuttle was launched into space. At first the ride was really bumpy, but it settled down once the shuttle left Earth's atmosphere.

All of a sudden, Janie heard a voice coming from the computer. "So, tell me what you see!" it said.

"Joey! How…?" Janie exclaimed to her friend's face on the computer.

"I told you I'd see you soon," Joey said. "Now tell me what you see out the window."

"Earth looks really pretty from up here," said Janie. "We've just flown past the moon. Wow! I've never seen the back side of the moon before."

Before Janie knew it, Earth had vanished from view, and the sun looked like just another star.

"It's amazing to see all the changing patterns the stars make as we zoom past," she told Joey. "I think I just saw Ursa Major. That's the **constellation** that looks like a bear."

"Hmm," said Joey. "If my calculations are correct, you're very close to Nina."

Joey was right. It wasn't long before they reached Nina. The spacecraft settled into **orbit** around the **planet.** The SPACER 3000 would fly around the planet twice before landing.

"What's it like?" Joey asked eagerly.

"I'm sending pictures to you right now," said Janie. "Wait until you see—Nina's colors are beautiful!"

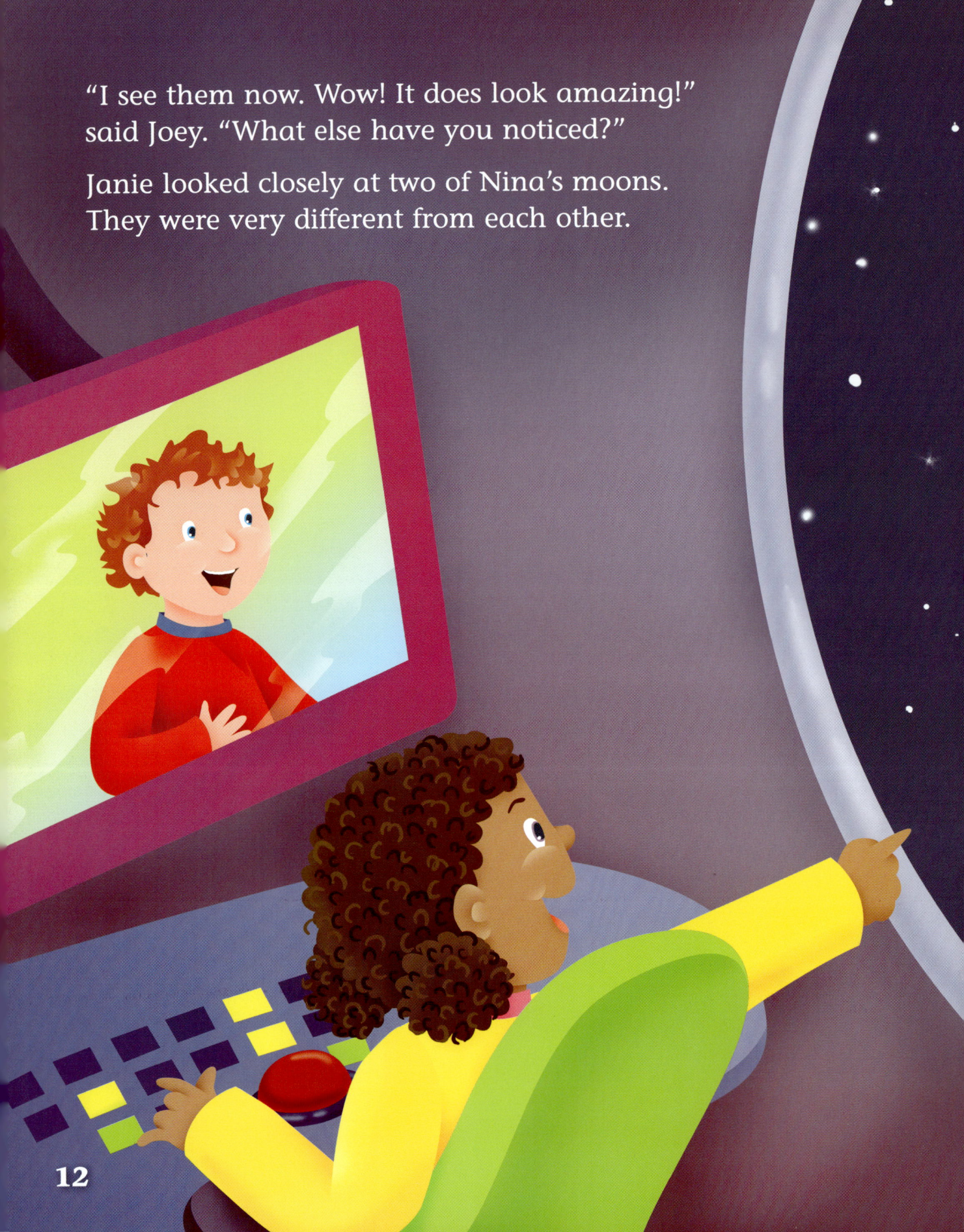

"I see them now. Wow! It does look amazing!" said Joey. "What else have you noticed?"

Janie looked closely at two of Nina's moons. They were very different from each other.

"One of Nina's moons is just a ball of rock, like Earth's moon. But another one is blue and green, just like Earth. I wonder if it has water and plants too."

"This is going to be a great year!" said Janie. "And the best part is that you will be moving up here soon, Joey!"

Earth Science
Nonfiction

Earth in Space

Spinning in Space

We are in space! You and all the people you know live on Earth. Earth is a **planet**. Planets are in space.

The sun, the moon, other stars, planets, and smaller objects like comets, asteroids, and small rocks are all found in space.

Earth Moves Around

The planet Earth does not just float in one spot in space. Earth is moving! Earth spins like a top. It takes 24 hours, or one full day, for Earth to make one complete turn on its **axis**. As Earth rotates, the side facing the sun experiences day, while the side facing away from the sun experiences night.

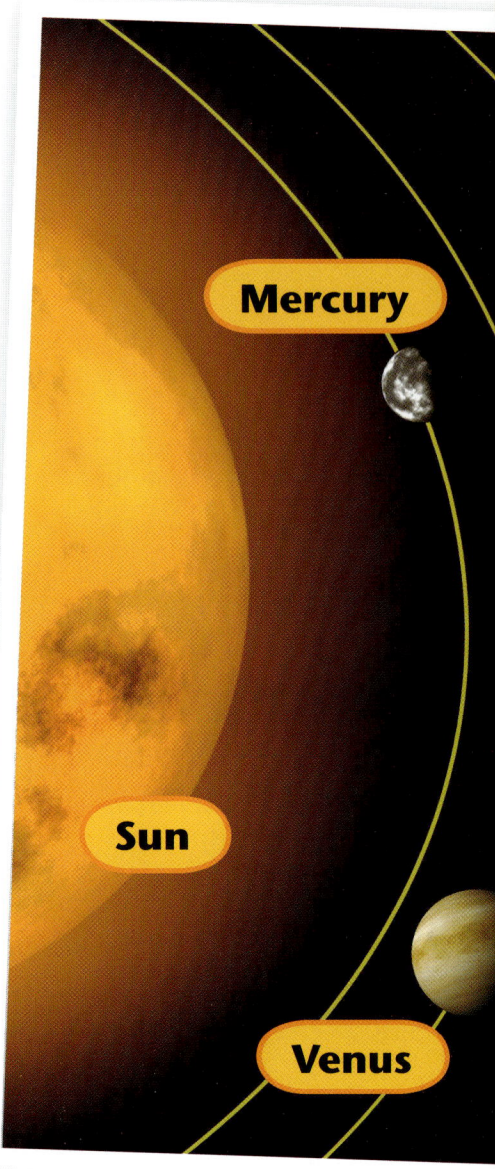

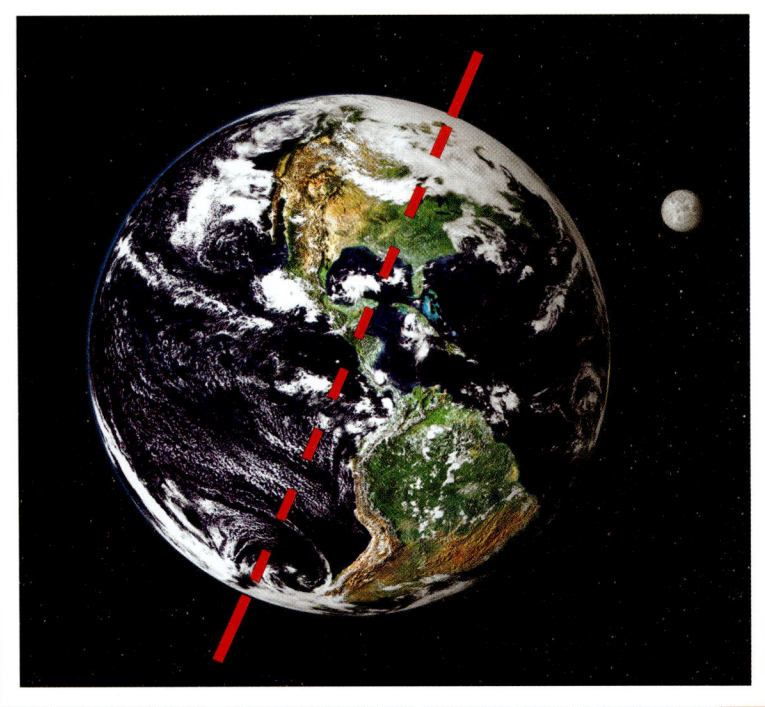

An axis is an imaginary line that runs through the center of a spinning object.

Earth also moves around the sun. Earth takes about 365 days to **orbit**, or move around, the sun. This means Earth takes about one year to make a complete trip. Earth is one of eight planets that orbit the sun.

The Reason for the Seasons

If you look carefully, you will see that Earth's axis is not straight up-and-down. Earth's axis is tilted. This tilt is the reason we have different seasons.

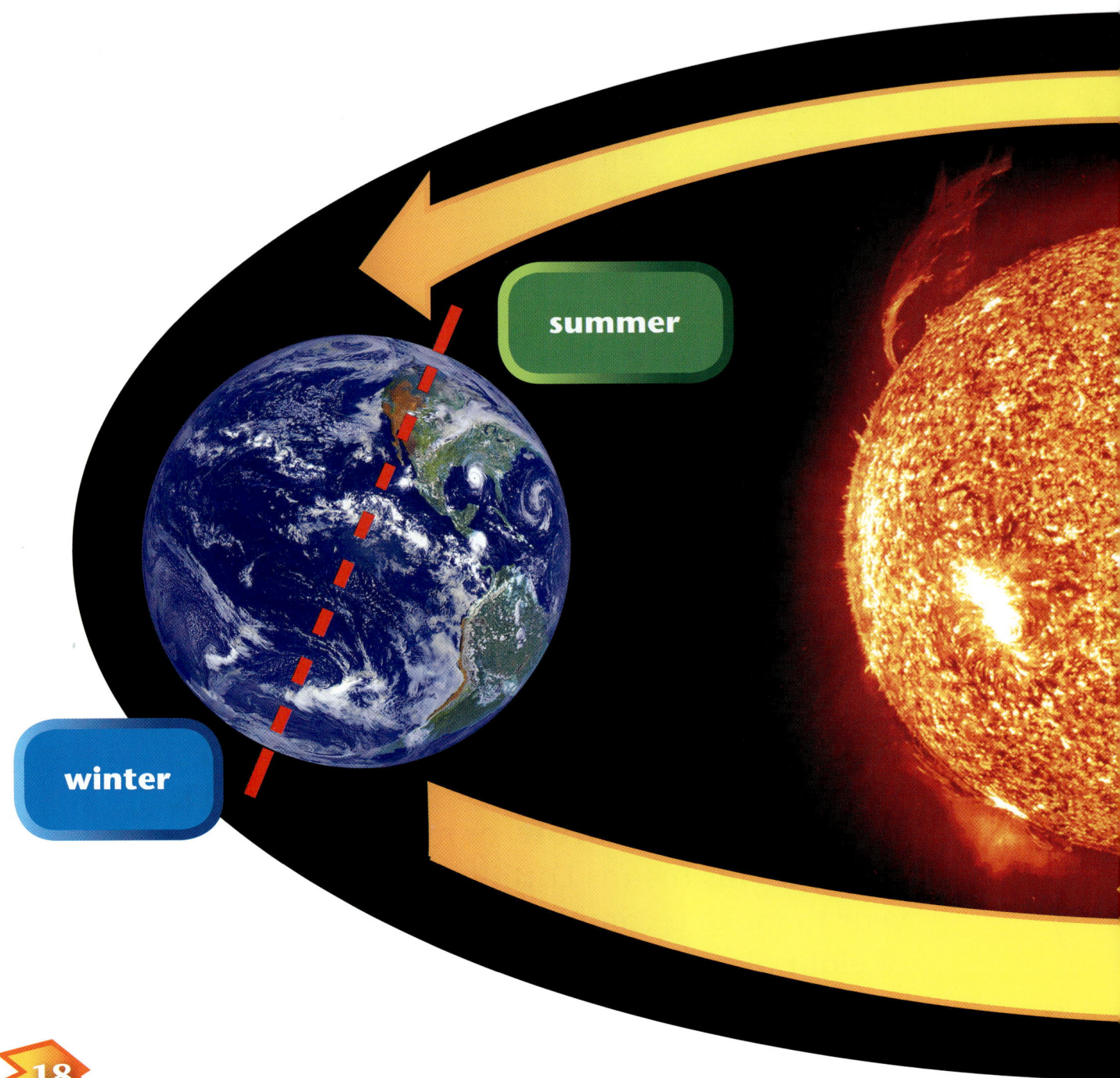

When the top half of Earth is tilted toward the sun, it is summer in that part of the world. When the top half of Earth is tilted away from the sun, it is winter there.

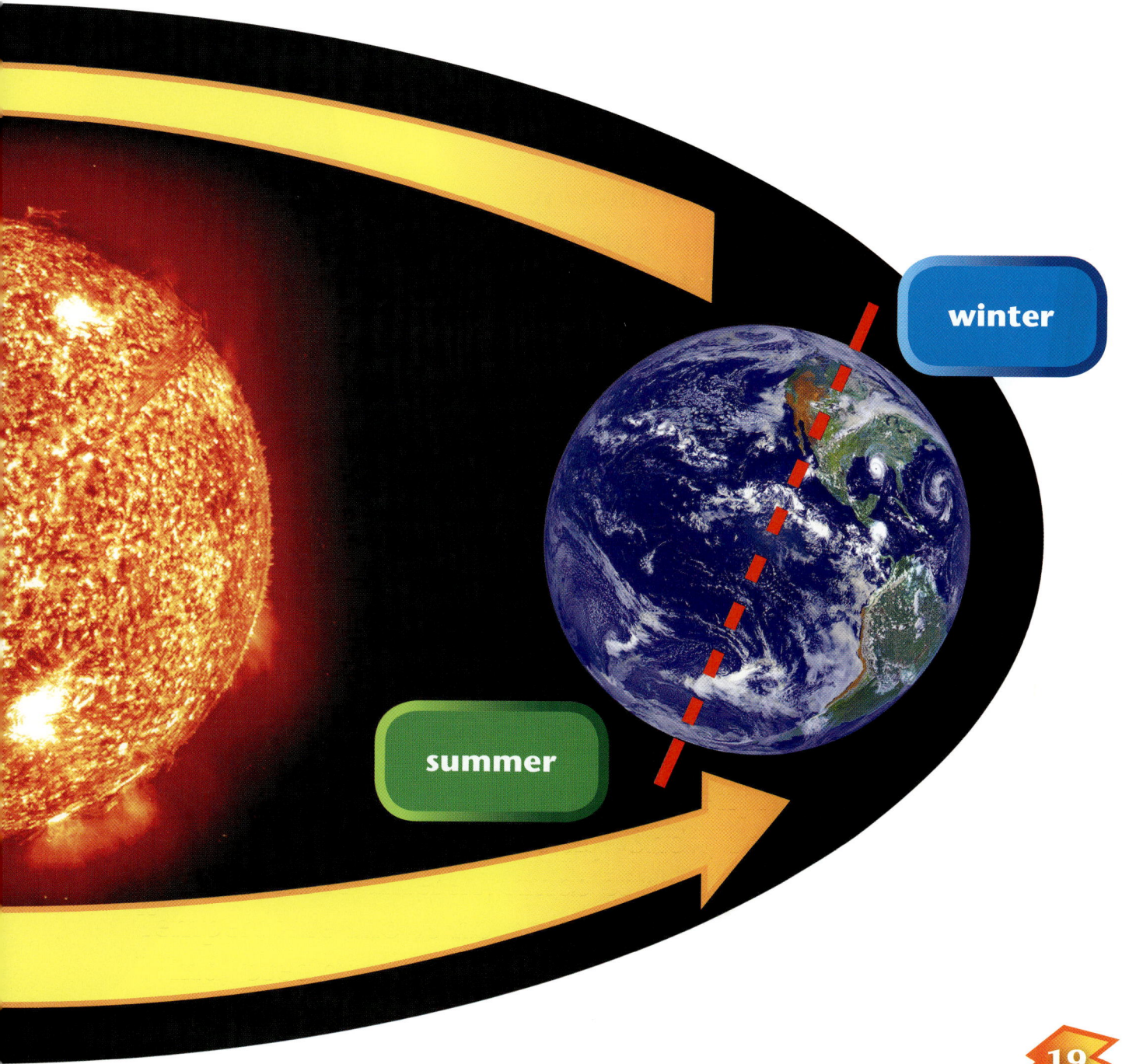

The Moon Moves Too

The moon orbits Earth just as Earth orbits the sun. The moon makes one complete trip around Earth about every 28 days.

The moon does not give off its own light. We see the moon shine because it **reflects** light from the sun. Because of the way the moon moves around Earth, we see the moon as different shapes at different times of the month. These shapes are called phases. During different phases, we see different amounts of the sunlit side of the moon.

> It takes about one month for the moon to go through all of its phases.

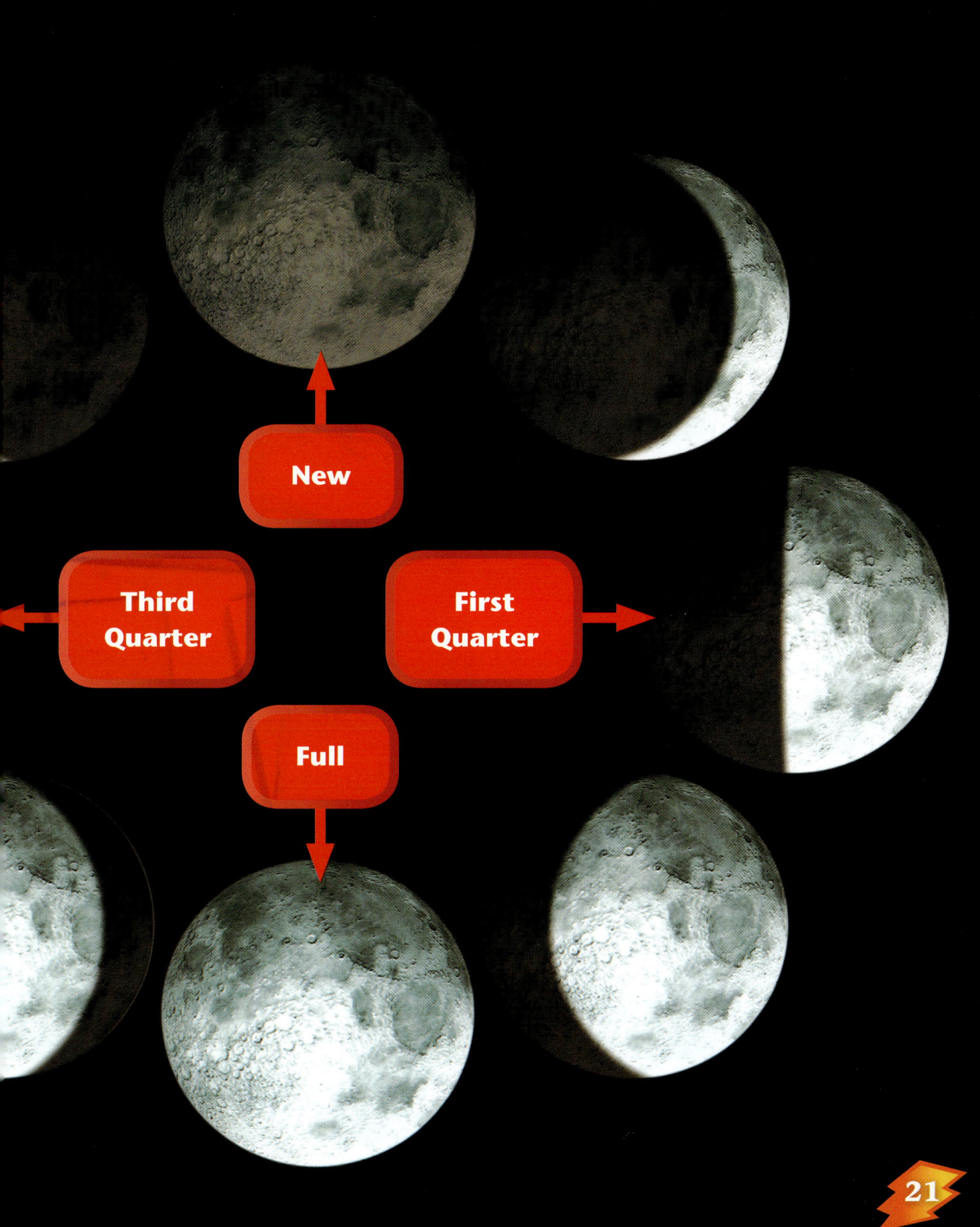

Little Star, Big Star

The sun is a star. Like all stars, it gives off its own **light**. On a clear night, you can see many tiny dots of light. These dots are also stars. They are very far from Earth. For centuries, people have imagined that groups of stars look like pictures. These star groups are called **constellations**.

This constellation is called Orion. It was named for a great hunter in Greek mythology.

Some of these faraway stars are like the sun. They are yellow-orange and medium-sized. Other stars are much bigger than the sun. Some of these big stars are a deep red color. Other stars are much smaller than the sun. These small stars can burn bright white, and they are very hot.

Art Credits

4–13 Robin Boyer

Photo Credits

14–15 © Royalty-Free/CORBIS; **15**(l) © Dennis di Cicco/CORBIS; **15**(tr) © NASA/Roger Ressmeyer/CORBIS; **15**(br) NASA; **16** © NASA/CORBIS; **16–17** © Tim Kiusalaas/CORBIS; **18** NASA; **18–19** © Brand X Pictures/PunchStock; **19** NASA; **20–21** © Victor Habbick Visions/Photo Researchers, Inc.; **22** NASA; **23** © PhotoDisc/Getty Images, Inc.